Copyright 2018 by TMR Group, Inc.

All rights reserved. No part of this publication may be reproduced, distributed, or transmitted in any form or by any means, including photocopying, recording, or other electronic or mechanical methods without the prior written permission of the organization.

For permission requests, solicit the organization online at www.GradPrep.org

Printed in the United States of America

CONTENTS

PART 1

1. YOUR CALLING — 1
2. YOUR CAREER — 9
3. YOUR COLLEGE — 18

PART 2

4. CAPABILITY — 25
5. COLLABORATION — 31
6. CHARACTER — 35

APPENDIX
APPLICATION GUIDE — 40

- PERSONAL STATEMENT — 41
- RÉSUMÉ BUILDER — 42
- RECOMMENDER PACKAGE — 49
- ESSAYS — 53
- ABOUT THE AUTHOR — 55
- ABOUT GRADPREP — 55

YOUR CALLING

So, you're thinking about going to graduate school?

Well, this is a great start.

You see, navigating that journey will involve loads of introspection, lots of writing and reading, and probably more than your fair share of coffee.

But, you want to do it. You *have* to do it. Right? It's this goal you have and you want those letters after your name. It looks so - *professional. Accomplished.*

You see, if you've convinced yourself and others that now is the time to do it, you'll need a support team. You'll need some tools … like this book.

I want to be one of your greatest coaches. I want to see you get into the best school for you, and I want your soul to be intact before, during, and after the process. Why?

I've traveled that road and it can be lonely at times. Having the right team on your side is key.

So, let's get started.

In this book, we'll go over your life from the end to where you are presently and find out where graduate school fits into the grand scheme of things. This is called backward-mapping, first introduced by a professor named Richard Elmore back in 1979.

> *We'll go over your life from the end to where you are presently and find out where graduate school fits into the grand scheme of things.*

YOUR CALLING

Your Calling: Passion And Purpose

First, let's do a visualization.

Close your eyes and picture your life when you're 80 years old. When you look back on your life, what do you see?

_____

_____

_____

This is an important visual of your legacy. Hopefully, you see how you've impacted the world and you're surrounded by people who love you. At the end of your journey, the people that have crossed your path will most likely forget you have a graduate degree; they will only remember how you treated them. They will only remember how they felt while interacting with you.

At the end of your journey, the people that have crossed your path will most likely forget you have a graduate degree; they will only remember how you treated them. They will only remember how they felt while interacting with you.

This is why it's so important to live your life according to your Calling, because then, and only then, will you truly be happy enough to give out hugs and high fives to people that cross your path. You'll be in alignment, and that's when things start to fall into place, and your heart beats with passion when you wake up in the morning.

Next, let's do Exercise 1. We're going to figure out your Calling based on your passion and purpose. Using the worksheet, *Identify Your Calling,* I want you to fill out your Calling according to what you feel your purpose is for your life. Purpose is what you do for other people. We are all here to use our skills to serve and help others.

In this worksheet, you'll also begin to think about your passions. As I said, passion is what gets you out of bed in the morning. Passion is what you do with or without compensation because you absolutely love doing it!

However, this workbook will actually walk you through steps to achieve **convergence** - that's when you make money doing what you love.

Once you finish this exercise, you'll have a sense of what your Calling is. Play soft music and find a quiet, comfortable area to do some soul searching on this. No distractions. Once you're done with this worksheet, we'll have the first tool to add to our toolkit on this journey.

YOUR CALLING

IDENTIFY YOUR CALLING - EXERCISE 1

PEOPLE	PASSION	PLACE
_____	_____	_____
_____	_____	_____
_____	_____	_____
_____	_____	_____
_____	_____	_____
_____	_____	_____
_____	_____	_____
_____	_____	_____
_____	_____	_____
_____	_____	_____

Instructions:

- Your PASSIONS are the center of your life CALLING.
- We are all called to use our skills to help certain people located in certain places. These people are your "sphere of influence."

1. PASSION: Starting in the middle category, "Passion," list out the first 7 words that come to mind that encompass what you are passionate about.
2. PEOPLE: Now, for each passion, list the type of people that will be affected by that particular passion in the "People" category.
3. PLACE: Where are the majority of these people located? List the location under the category "Place."

Once you finish this worksheet, you will have a list of the types of people you are called to and a sense of their locations.

YOUR CALLING

You have now identified your life CALLING.

You are now ready to write your life purpose statements here by filling in the blank sections of this sentence:

Example: I am called to use my passion of _____ to help _____ located in _____.

_____

_____

_____

_____

_____

Note: We all have more than one purpose, so you will have more than one sentence. Once you complete all of the sentences according to your list above, you will have a complete paragraph.

Please write out your paragraph here, adding on to the life purpose statements with more details, as you wish.

I am called to use my passion of....

_____

_____

_____

_____

_____

_____

YOUR CALLING

Conquering Fear

Now you have a macro level view of your Calling as it pertains to your purpose and passions. It's exhilarating, but a bit scary, yes? After all, others before you have chosen more traditional paths in their career, and stayed on that course their entire life.

Life is a fantastic adventure filled with pit stops along the way. We are faced with choices. When we decide on a choice, that process is either based on fear or it is based on love.

When you are passionate about using your unique talents and skills to help others, you are choosing outcomes based on love. Perfect love drives out fear.

Let's face these fears we may have in our internal decision-making process. As you work through the questions, you will find where most of your motivation rests when you make decisions: avoidance of pain (Prevent Pain) or hope of progress (Pursue Gain).

Your Motivation - Pursue Gain vs. Prevent Pain

In the book *Decide* by Steve McClatchy, the author discusses the findings from psychologists about human motivation. Our decisions are basically categorized into two motivating forces: to Pursue Gain or to Prevent Pain.

Pursue Gain are choices we make to grow and live life in our higher Calling. They are choices we do not have to do, therefore, Pursue Gain differentiates you from other people.

Our decisions are basically categorized into two motivating forces: to Pursue Gain or to Prevent Pain.

A great example of Pursue Gain is your motivation for pursuing your graduate degree. Although it is not usually a requirement to get a job in life, it may qualify a person in the longer run for higher level, higher paying jobs and projects. In fact, some occupations require a master's degree for entry level jobs.

Additionally, the connections you make while in school and, afterwards through the alumni network, broadens your sphere of influence.

Let's continue to ponder for a moment on your motivations for pursuing a graduate degree. This exercise will not only reflect your personal motivations, but also help craft your Purpose Statement, Essays and Interview later on in this book, and during the graduate admissions process.

> 💡 In general, why are you pursuing a degree?
> _____
> _____

YOUR CALLING

Table 1 - Pursue Gain

List 5 **personal** reasons you are pursuing a graduate degree on the left. (impact self)

List 5 **service** reasons you are pursuing a graduate degree on the right. (impact others)

Impact Self	Impact Others
1.	1.
2.	2.
3.	3.
4.	4.
5.	5.

As you review the impact you could make through your college program, you will begin to see the significance involved when we conquer fear, and choose to live our life based on our Calling.

Conquer Fear - Worst Case Scenario

Choosing the greater path means you will be a trailblazer. For some, this is exhilarating and life-giving. You will jump right in with bright eyes and seemingly endless strength down the road marked "Adventure." During that discovery process, you'll find the treasure is not in the destination, but in the journey.

For others, you stand at the crossroads of "Adventure" and "Comfort." There are usually two types of fear that grip people at the beginning - *fear of failure* and *fear of success.*

Your choice will begin with your thoughts. Your mind will reveal visions of both failure and success. What would be the worst case scenario if you chose this action? Leon Seltzer, PhD. further discusses this model in *Psychology Today*.[1]

When we figure out what the worst case scenario would be in any given situation, and the odds of it happening, this will help alleviate some of that fear as you pursue, "Adventure."

Conquer Fear - Micro-Actions

One of the best ways to conquer fear is through "micro-actions". These daily, consistent steps are small in nature but big on building your confidence. You will be challenged to take these steps later in the Career section of this workbook.

Conquer Fear - Shades of Gray

Another effective way to conquer fear is to change your perception of failure. Let's assign "complete failure," the color black, a "complete success," the color white, and, "somewhere in the middle of that spectrum," a shade of gray.

Using the Conquering Fear Milestones worksheet, next, fill out areas in your life where you have hesitated to step out and conquer due to fear, uncertainty or other factors. List those on the left.

Next, record what happened when you took a small step towards overcoming that fear. Was this black, white or a gray area? What lessons did you learn by taking action? Was this a win for you by sparking a new best practice, idea or zeal to take the next step? Record your milestones.

Truth is, the only way you fail is by completely giving up. It sounds trite, but if you perceive life as a learning process, where one decision along your path will give you lessons needed for the next fork in the road, you will see there is no reason to fear.

Determining your Calling is part of the process, however, conquering fear will determine your destination.

---

1 Seltzer, L. (2018). *2 Keys for Conquering Your Worst Case Scenarios.* [online] Psychology Today. Available at: https://www.psychologytoday.com/intl/blog/evolution-the-self/201601/2-keys-conquering-your-worst-case-scenarios [Accessed 14 Nov. 2018].

YOUR CALLING

CONQUERING FEAR MILESTONES

Date	What happened?	Black, white, grey	Lesson learned	New model best practice
1.				
2.				
3.				
4.				
5.				
6.				
7.				
8.				
9.				

YOUR CAREER

Okay, you made it through Step 1.

Let's sit and have a coffee chat for a sec.

A lot of people think when they graduate from college, they have a particular career path they will take. In all actuality, that hardly ever happens.

According to the Bureau of Labor Statistics, a longitudinal study conducted on Baby Boomers born between 1957 and 1964 revealed that both men and women held, on average, *11 jobs* between the ages of 18 and 48. People take a lot of twists and turns, there are forks in the road, and decisions need to be made. Many times, we walk paths in the future that we would have never thought of choosing.

This happens for several reasons. One reason is because a certain job you may have to take may not be a life career path, but it will build your character. Later on, we'll talk about character in more detail and why it's important to sustain your relationships, your brand, and your reputation.

There are certain skills you will obtain in a particular job during a life season. Those skills will become part of your toolkit. Please remember, *there are no wasted seasons.* Every job you have, everything you learn, you will use that wisdom later on in your life. I guarantee you.

Please remember, there are no wasted seasons. Every job you have, everything you learn, you will use that wisdom later on in your life.

YOUR CAREER

So, at one point, I was working in an Alzeheimer's care center. Mind you, it was never a desire of mine to work in the health field, let alone with the elderly. I had a degree in fashion merchandising and a Masters in Public Administration. My next goal was ministry school, and I had to pay the bills somehow while in Redding, California.

The only job that opened up was caregiver. *Noc shifts, scrubs and tons of laundry.* I learned so much from that job. I may not have made a lot of money, but what was learned was used later on, particularly with my grandmother and mother-in-law, who both had dementia. It was comforting to be able to take care of them for a while and help with self-care. These are skills I would have never known had I not taken on that job during that life season.

So, yes, sometimes we have to sacrifice.

Pride and ego are deficit energies that will become stumbling blocks if we let them. I had to let both of those go so many times in exchange for humility. Over time, it became apparent that everything we do serves a greater purpose - and that is to help other people.

There's something very fulfilling in serving and focusing on other people rather than just ourselves. Have you noticed whenever you help someone else, you end up getting help in the process? It's pretty cool how that works out.

Over time, it became apparent that everything we do serves a greater purpose - and that is to help other people. There's something very fulfilling in serving and focusing on other people rather than just ourselves.

YOUR CAREER

Corporate, NGO or Entrepreneur?

When you think about your career, part of the process is thinking about the type of culture you would flourish in, and what type of company suits your values and your skill set.

Here are three general categories you can start off with: Corporate, Non-Governmental Organization (NGO), and Entrepreneur.

In the table below, Corporate is denoted with a triangle, which represents the culture of position and hierarchy. NGO/Non-Profit has a culture of hope symbolized with the heart. If you have the desire to be an entrepreneur, you flourish well in a culture of risk, represented with the star.

Let's take a look at the table.

Table 2 - Corporate, NGO or Entrepreneur

Corporate △	NGO/Non-Profit ♡	Entrepreneur ☆
position	*hope*	*risk*
structure	mission-driven	trailblazer
stability	impact	innovator
routine/predictability	change	driven
task-oriented	passionate	creative
clear goals/outcomes	justice	risk taker
manager	defender	visionary leader

Please start circling the words you are drawn to; they can be in any of the three different categories and columns. Don't focus on the category, moreso, the words that speak to your heart.

Once you're done circling, add up the circles in each column. The column that has the most circles in it is more likely the direction you're currently headed in.

I have worked in all three structures, so this is why I don't like to label people or put them into boxes. Here, you will be able to see where you are leaning towards currently, and this is a tool you can always reference in your journey to plan your next career move.

YOUR CAREER

The C.O.C. Method - How to Identify Innovative Companies

Did you have the most circles in the "Corporate" column? Are you relieved or concerned?

If you are concerned, more than likely, you circled many other words outside of this column and all you can see in your future are the walls of a cubicle surrounding you like a coffin.

If you are relieved, you feel comfortable and peaceful in such a predictable setting.

Either way, I have a tool for you called The C.O.C. method. The C.O.C. method stands for, "C-Suite, Opportunities and Culture." You can actually choose corporations that suit your need to make an impact through The C.O.C. method.

Whether you are an entry level employee or at the executive level, exploring opportunities through a search firm, the simplest way to identify innovative companies that embrace dynamic diversity is through The C.O.C. Method.

Change can come from the bottom up, or by trickling down.

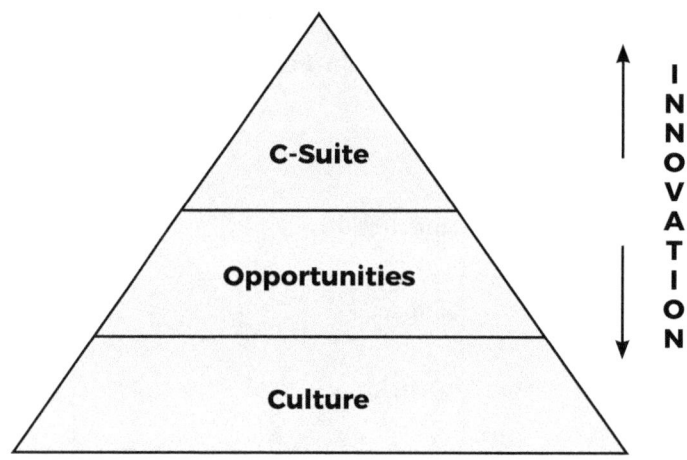

The C.O.C. Method Pyramid

- **CULTURE:** Determining your personal fit is first achieved by identifying the company's culture. Is it conservative or progressive? Traditional corporate hierarchy or flat-model? Do they have work/life programs and community service initiatives? What about a triple bottom line approach to business?
- **OPPORTUNITIES:** Are there training programs in place to aid in your professional development? What about affinity and culture programs to find internal mentors and network outside of office hours? Are there rotational programs and/or advancement roadmaps?
- **C-SUITES:** Take a look up top, at the C-suites. If they are diverse, there is a strong chance that your efforts up the ladder will not be in vain. Also, take note of the top level's approach towards product/service development.

YOUR CAREER

The Holland Codes

Be encouraged to dig deeper in this process to find a niche that works perfectly for you. For further self-directed study, I recommend the Holland Codes, which are based on John L. Holland's research of six personality types of job seekers. You can simply Google "Holland Codes Quiz" and take it online. Write your answers below:

I scored highest in_____, second highest in _____. My Holland Code is _____.

Job clusters include: _____

_____

_____

_____

Career Goal Mapping

Using the **Career Goal Chart** (on page 16) as a reference, your next assignment is to fill in the micro-actions for Mentorship, Volunteer, Internship and/or Pro-bono.

You will choose the category (-ies) that make sense to you right now to conquer fear and move forward.

Mentorship

I highly suggest choosing mentorship as one of the categories. You want to serve under someone who has already blazed trails, who you respect and who inspires you. Motivation and success are contagious. You will have access to their wisdom and sphere of influence if you follow protocol, honor, and serve well.

The basic steps to securing a mentor are as follows:
1. Identify
2. Research potential mentor's background
3. Read their books, blogs, etc.
4. Contact the potential mentor to offer service
5. Serve
6. Branch out and/or partner when ready

Action: Fill out the Career Goal Chart under the Mentorship category. Be sure to set a deadline for each action.

YOUR CAREER

Volunteer ♡

If you feel called to NGO and non-profit organizations, volunteerism is a great way to learn about the business side of a cause. You can maintain your current job and volunteer on the weekends, part-time, and/or evenings to help a mission move forward, while also determining if this path is for you.

To move forward into volunteerism:
1. Select organization
2. Inquire of volunteer needs
3. If good fit, serve
4. Build relationships
5. Build experience and reputation - consistency is key
6. Collaborate or start your own organization when ready

Action: Fill in the Volunteer category and add deadlines for each action.

Internship △

Internships are an excellent way to gain experience and build your résumé. Use The C.O.C. Model to select a company that would be a good fit for you.

To succeed as an intern:
1. Select company
2. Research their products, services, and leadership
3. Understand and memorize their vision and mission statement
4. Know their milestones and backstory
5. Research their internship program
6. Contact/build relationship
7. Begin internship

Action: Fill in the Internship section and add deadlines for each action.

YOUR CAREER

Pro-bono service

If you are an emerging entrepreneur, pro-bono service will build your business as you serve the community. This is an option for those who need to take micro-actions to build confidence and credibility before taking the complete leap into full-time entrepreneurship. Take these steps at your own pace.

To offer this aspect of your business:
1. Serve another business
2. Build clients and experience (referrals and testimonies from current job)
3. Gather video testimonies, recommendations, photography for your own brand
4. Build your brand by connecting through social media (Facebook (FB) group, Instagram, blog, etc.)
5. Monetize your own service when ready

Action: Fill in the Pro-bono section and add deadlines and ideas for each action.

The main takeaway from this section is to take small steps forward. There are no clear, sure career paths, and everyone's approach to meaningful work is different. Hopefully, these exercises and challenges will spark creativity and challenge you to become accountable in your journey.

Additional Career resources (Google them!):
1. Myers Briggs
2. Strong Interest Inventory Exam
3. Act's World of Work Map[2]

---

2 Visit http://www.act.org for more information

YOUR CAREER

CAREER GOAL CHART

Mentorship

1. Identify — Connection? / Respect? / Inspiration?
2. Research background
3. Read their books/blogs/content
4. Contact — Refer to #1 if factors still standing, proceed.
5. Serve
6. Branch out and / or partner when Ready

Volunteer

1. Select organization
2. Inquire Of Need
3. If Good fit, serve
4. Build relationship(s)
5. Build experience & reputation (consistency is KEY)
6. Collaborate or start own organization when ready

Internship

1. Select Company
2. Research — Leadership / Services / Product
3. Understand their vision & mission
4. Know Milestones & backstory
5. Research internship program
6. Contact/build relationship
7. Intern – determine FIT

Pro-bono

1. Serve
2. Build clients & experience — referrals / testimonies
3. Gather
   - video testimonies
   - recommendations
   - photography
4. Social Media — blog / Snapchat / Instagram / FB Group
5. Monetize — Subscribe/membership fee / Monetize blog / CDs/DVDs / books / ebooks / Online workshops / Offline speaking

YOUR CAREER

Mentorship

Deadline

1. Identify Mentor ☐
2. Research / Keypoints ☐
   a) _____
   b) _____
   c) _____
3. Read Mentor's Book ☐
4. Contact Mentor ☐
5. Serve ☐
6. Branch out / partner ☐

Volunteer

Deadline

1. Select company ☐
2. Inquire of Needs ☐
3. Serve ☐
4. Build relationship(s) ☐
5. Consistency ☐
6. Collaborate or start my own organization ☐

Intern

Deadline

1. Select Company ☐
2. Research ☐
   _____
   _____
3. Memorize Vision / Mission ☐
4. Milestones ☐
5. Research internship program ☐
6. Contact / Build relationships ☐
7. Begin Internship ☐

Pro-Bono

Deadline

1. Serve ☐
2. Build clients / experience ☐
3. Gather videos / testimonies ☐
4. Build your brand ☐
   a) Facebook
   b) Instagram
   c) Blog
5. Monetize ☐
   a) _____
   b) _____
   c) _____

YOUR COLLEGE

So, now that you have a clear vision of your *why*, it's time to figure out what the best program is for you to get there.

First, let's view the overall checklist titled, "Application Checklist." You can refer to this during the process for each school/program.

Now, back to school selection. There are some variables that I would like for you to consider, and you are free to add your own to this. They are:
- Curriculum
- Community
- Campus
- Cost

Curriculum

What programs offer the best curriculum that aligns with your learning style and career interests?

Let us start by doing your research.
Information gathering is critical because you will need a baseline to build on. Once you visit program websites to check some items off your checklist, next you will need to schedule campus visits to narrow down your choices.

Fit is extremely important. If you attend a program, and you are unable to connect with your professors and colleagues, it's going to be a painful experience.

YOUR COLLEGE

APPLICATION CHECKLIST

1. Apply for FAFSA (to increase aid, apply by the earliest deadline) at https://studentaid.ed.gov/sa/fafsa
2. Take entrance exam (GRE, LSAT, GMAT, MCAT, etc.)
3. Note any pre-requisites required for programs and complete
4. Narrow down schools to five (5)
5. Schedule school visits (prospective student day and regular day, if possible)
6. Meet professors, students and alumni - keep in touch. (Choose one (1) for mock interview; incorporate your experience with them in your essay and/or statement of purpose)
7. Order transcripts
8. Choose recommenders (academic, professional, community)
9. Note application rounds/deadlines
10. Note scholarship rounds/deadlines. Apply. #TeamDebtFree
11. Note Financial Aid deadlines for each school. Apply. #TeamDebtFree
12. Résumé/Curriculum Vitae (CV)
13. Write statement of purpose and essays for each school
14. Send Recommendation (Rec) Package to recommenders
15. Apply to your top five (5) schools

Once accepted:
- [ ] Secure housing
- [ ] Transportation
- [ ] Food
- [ ] Work-study
- [ ] Part-time job
- [ ] Get books for class

YOUR COLLEGE

Knowing your learning style is critical. If you are more of a hands-on, tactile learner, and a program only offers Innovations in Science in an auditory, lecture-style format, then be prepared for naptime.

You can use the *College Metric Worksheet* to fill in the information.

Community

Community is comprised of factors such as fit, challenge, colleagues, alumni, and extracurriculars.

Fit is extremely important. I cannot stress this enough. If you attend a program, and you are unable to connect with your professors and colleagues, it is going to be a painful experience. I do not want you to have any regrets.

You will only know this if you actually put in the time to visit the school, conquer fear, and start conversations with people on campus.

Do the people generally look happy? Do you feel challenged by the conversations with professors and students? In general, does your heart come alive walking around? Take note of your experience at each school.

- *A word on prospective student days ...*
Please do not just "go" to this event! It's similar to dating.
 The first date everyone is on best behavior. You want to be sure to visit on a regular day. Sit in on a class. See if people are responsive and friendly towards you. It will give you a more realistic gauge of campus culture and if you love the community.

- *A word on extracurricular activities ...*
Are you active? What are your favorite sports? Hobbies? If the extras are important to you, talk to the coaches, the athletes and go to a game. Going the extra mile to experience this part of campus life can be a deal-breaker, and help you make a final decision on the program that's best for you.

- *And finally, a word on alumni ...*
You can usually find out how to reach alumni through the program website. Set up a few informational interviews with alumni that have walked down your career path. Take notes on their experiences. If they make time for you, this is a strong indicator of alumni engagement and will be a mark in this program's favor in your selection process.

Campus

The campus location you choose can be online, local, and abroad. If you have a full-time job, perhaps an online or evening program is better for your needs. If you love travel and new cultures, a program abroad will be a memorable experience for you and stretch your learning to new dimensions.

YOUR COLLEGE

As you know, a local program would not be able to offer you much adventure, but it may be more cost-effective for you.

So, weigh in on your options and consider factors like family, current job, and finances to choose the best campus setting within your parameters.

Cost

The focus of the Cost section will be called **#TeamDebtFree**, because my greatest piece of advice to you is to <u>avoid student debt</u>. This means avoiding student loans and living within your budget. This singular piece of advice will bring you peace of mind if you follow it.

For those who love equations:

BUDGETING - STUDENT LOANS = PEACE

No one was there to mentor me about phrases like *opportunity cost* and how to calculate *compound daily interest rates* on my student loans.

The cost to apply to a program will include some or all of the following:
- application fee
- test prep fee
- tuition
- books
- student housing/food
- travel to/from school

> **#TeamDebtFree**
>
> Frederick Towles, M.B.A. of The Towles Group recommends 3 tips:
> 1. Apply for FAFSA as early as possible.
> 2. Stay away from credit cards.
> 3. Stay on the budget after you create it.

Next Steps:

1. In your *College Metric Worksheet,* there is a place for you to put the total cost for each program.
2. In your *#TeamDebtFree Worksheet,* you can calculate final cost after aspects like fellowships, scholarships, and grants have reduced the program cost. **Eliminate any programs that will cause you to get loans, to live outside of your budget, or cause any sort of financial pressure long or short term.**
3. Use the Budget Template for College Student to help you create a budget.

Action: Use the checklist, metric worksheets, and budget to finalize your program selection. Refer to these throughout the process, filling in more details as you research and complete each line item.

Other College resources:

In the Appendix section, there is a bonus College Application Guide. You are also able to go to GradPrep.org to download additional free templates.

YOUR COLLEGE

College Metric Worksheet

Name of College	Rank	Curriculum	Community	Campus	*Total Cost	Other Notes	Deadline
example: University Of Southern California (USC)	1	hybrid	diverse, strong alumni network	L.A., Sacramento and online	$77,663 for 2 year program	numerous scholarships available. https://priceschool.usc.edu/students/financial-aid/	March 1st

#TeamDebtFree

School Name	Rank	Savings	Financial Aid Package	Scholarships	Work-Study	Other (grants, fellowships, fundraising efforts, etc.)	Debt-Free?

Budget Template College Student

Income For Month Of : _____

Item	Amount
Monthly Income	
Financial Awards	
Allowance	
Other Income	
Total	

Expenses for Month of: _____

Item	Amount
Housing	
Insurance	
Utilities	
Groceries	
Phone	
Loans, Student	
Credit Cards	
Medical	
Entertainment	
Laundry	
Miscellaneous	
Total	

Semester Costs For Month Of: _____

Item	Amount
Tuition	
Books	
Lab Fees	
Transportation	
Deposits	
Other	
Total	

Overall View

Item	Amount
Monthly Income	
Monthly Expenses	
Semester Expenses	
Difference	

PART 2

THE 3 C'S: CAPABILITY, COLLABORATION, AND CHARACTER

In Part 2 of this workbook, you will read the stories of three alumni who faced life challenges internationally. You may identify with some or all of their challenges. The questions at the end of each interview will challenge you to take actions that implement The 3 C's model: Capability, Collaboration, and Character.

CAPABILITY

In the book *Originals,* by Adam Grant, the author shares his definition of originality. In his words, "Originality is rejecting the default and exploring whether better options exist."

Let's take this concept even further and apply it in context to capability.

There are benefits of being innovative and not conforming to the norm.

You are an original. You are capable. You have a Calling to be and do something like no other on this earth. Our fingerprints are unique, yet why do many of us settle into conformity?

We read about the child prodigies who are able to solve complex calculus equations and play Mozart arrangements at the age of three. That little kid has a way with the piano; why not challenge him to design his own arrangement?

How can you use your creativity to design something that *has not been imagined or implemented yet?*

How can you use your capability to take something that already exists and make it better?

CAPABILITY

Accomplishments, Learning and Radical Risks

Many times we fear failure and we value achievement.

I think we have the wrong connotation of failure. The only way we fail is if we quit. Otherwise, we are learning. Let us replace failure with the word *learning*.

If we aim to learn through unique accomplishments instead of guaranteed success, we become our most authentic selves.

We tend to believe that the definition of achievement is the perfection of something that already exists. Let us challenge this and expand our mindset.

What if the highest level of achievement is when you create something new? The world will then have a better solution available because you were courageous enough to go against the grain and to seek other options. In other words, to be an original, according to Adam Grant, you need to take "radical risks".

The Gordian Knot

The "gordian knot" is a term applied to a seemingly complex, insolvable problem. Let us take a quick coffee break and read about this legend.

As the story goes, in 333 B.C., the Macedonian conqueror marched his army into the Phrygian capital of Gordium in modern day Turkey. Upon arriving in the city, he encountered an ancient wagon, with its yoke tied with, what one Roman historian later described as, "several knots all so tightly entangled that it was impossible to see how they were fastened."

Phrygian tradition held that the wagon had once belonged to Gordius, the father of the celebrated King Midas. An oracle had declared that any man who could unravel its elaborate knots was destined to become ruler of all of Asia.

According to the ancient chronicler Arrian, the impetuous Alexander was instantly "seized with an ardent desire" to untie the Gordian knot. After wrestling with it for a time, and finding no success, he stepped back from the mass of gnarled ropes and proclaimed, "It makes no difference how they are loosed." He then drew his sword and sliced the knot in half with a single stroke.[3]

---

3. https://www.history.com/news/what-was-the-gordian-knot

CAPABILITY

Challenge:

1. What are some radical risks you can make in your personal and professional life?

   _____
   _____
   _____
   _____

2. How will these risks expand your capability in any given area of your life?

   _____
   _____
   _____
   _____

3. Do you see how personal risks translate into career risks *in a good way*? How so?

   _____
   _____
   _____
   _____

There is performance capital and there is social capital.

An opportunity was presented to me to move abroad because I had proven myself as someone who could thrive under challenging situations. I had gained performance capital – by continually seeking out challenges, and then accomplishing those goals or that kind of difficulty.

Social capital is when people speak highly of you; either they like you, and/or like your performance. As an example, if someone asked about you, when you are not in the room, the majority opinion is positive. When the opinion is positive, the opportunities will come to you.

"Doing and conquering gives you confidence ... and the anxiety, the doubting hesitation to jump at an opportunity, or to fail lessens ... because, ultimately, even if you've failed, then surely you've learned something." **- JONTE'**

COFFEE CHAT WITH JONTE'

Cultural Competence And Becoming The Expert

Question   Okay, so you've mentioned Hong Kong and these different places you've been to. My first question would be: how did you feel while there? Were you able to acclimate with time? If yes, how so?

JONTE'   I definitely knew I looked different! But my approach was to be present and competent. I introduced myself when I didn't know someone and greeted everyone. Yes, I needed to culturally acclimate. My first boss in Hong Kong was Singaporean. He was very meticulous. So rounded numbers didn't cut it. He wanted to know precisely. Interestingly, the same thing was true in Japan.

Often, to gain that degree of detail, I needed to ask a number of questions, but not let doubt hinder my confidence.

I learned that asking questions and getting to the answer allows you to move forward with true confidence. If you're not asking questions, you're not learning (or relearning). The pace of change in business due to technology and disruption means you have to continually learn, and ask questions. Learning never stops.

Question   Do you feel being humble has helped your learning curve?

JONTE'   Yes. Later on, I was in charge of all the Asia trading for my product. I was in

Australia, Indonesia, Thailand and Singapore. Business is done differently in each one and so it's important to ask the question, "Is this form okay?"

Meaning, you're effectively getting feedback from someone else, asking for help, not being afraid to say, "This may not be correct, I think I have it right, but, confirm this," ... but still being confident that you know what you're doing. That sometimes is difficult because some people think it's, "Oh, if I'm asking someone, it's not demonstrating what I know."

Question: **Do you have advice for both undergraduate and graduate students?**

JONTE' Yes, I think this actually can apply to both, which is, "sweat the small stuff and the details early."

For example, when you read an acronym, do you know what it means?

Most folks will generally gloss off over that acronym and continue reading. Often those acronyms hold a lot of value if you understand what they are.

You should not be afraid, whether you are a director at the bank or an analyst, to ask the question either verbally to a boss or to a peer, "What does this mean?" If they don't know the answer, that will clue you in that you're asking the right questions.

You find the answer, you become the expert.

So, if someone later asks you, "What does it mean?", you will be able to tell them, and then you will appear knowledgeable because *you are* knowledgeable.

CHALLENGE:

Identify a problem within your company or community. Ask questions to gather information. Find a solution and present it to your supervisor and/or the decision makers. Whether they implement your solution or not, use their feedback as a learning curve. Add this experience to your résumé builder milestones, and/or application essays.

Question **Can you describe a challenging situation in your career with your supervisor and how you overcame it?**

JONTE' Three weeks after I arrived in Hong Kong, my boss resigned and moved to a different bank. So, I had a new boss, in the same year I expected to be promoted to Vice President.

And so, despite the fact that I was chosen to move to Hong Kong because I was very good at my job, I had a new boss who didn't really know me, and couldn't really represent me in front of a promotion committee.

Having not been put up for promotion, I was furious. I called back to New York, to people I knew very well, who thought very highly of me, and I said, *"I'm resigning. Why would I have moved here when I would have been promoted in the U.S.?"*

My complaint set off this chain where everyone agreed that I should have been promoted, but understood why it wasn't proposed.

And so, it was agreed that I would be paid the same as if I've been promoted, but I'd receive the title a year later.

So, the lesson it taught me was that, if I had any fault in this situation, it was that I did not communicate my value to my new boss, so that he could confidently go into a meeting and say "This is what Jonte' is doing."

I had six months to show him all of my wins, but I had my head down thinking that he and others would naturally see my performance and effort.

Bottom line, it doesn't work like that. I needed to communicate my wins, and sometimes over-communicate them. From then on, I was intentionally vocal about my performance.

Question So, in that same vein, do you feel like you could have built a stronger connection with your new Australian boss?

JONTE' I did, and to this day, he is one of my professional advocates.

CHALLENGE:

Challenge: In the Appendix, the Application Guide includes a Recommender Package. Complete the steps to secure recommenders for school, eventually giving them your tailored Recommender Package. Note that the timeline for relationship-building starts 6 to 12 months in advance.

5

COLLABORATION

Collaboration is next. It is a subject we try to avoid because it is like ripping off a Band-Aid, over and over again. Why?

Because it is painful to keep running into people we deem difficult in social settings, work settings, and even within our family structures at times. They trigger us with annoyance, impatience, and frustration. We try to avoid them at all costs, but they are everywhere.

Well, let us try a different approach…

What happens if we change our perspective about "difficult people?"

What if we choose collaboration, and identify ways challenging situations can actually be beneficial to our own growth?

Dr. Nicolya Williams[4] and Certified Coaches Alliance (CCA)[5] developed an effective strategy to increase our capacity to collaborate.

> ***What if we choose collaboration, and identify ways challenging situations can actually be beneficial to our own growth?***

---

4 https://www.nicolyawilliams.com/

5 https://certifiedcoachesalliance.com/

COLLABORATION

Collaboration Exercise

1. **See difficult people as teachers.** They may be in your life to teach you a valuable lesson.
   - What can you learn from a difficult person in your life? What lessons can you pick up from interacting with this person? Even if it's only to teach you patience, they are valuable to you in some way.
   - Why does this person remain in your life?

   _____
   _____
   _____

2. **See difficult people as messengers.** Perhaps they are revealing to you a part of your personality that could use some work or healing. They may trigger thoughts and feelings in you that require some thought and soul searching.
   - For example, a person who annoys you with constant talking may be triggering the part of you that could work on communication. Why are you bothered by the extensive talking, and what does it really mean?

   _____
   _____
   _____

3. **Learn to change reactions.** If a difficult person can't be avoided, it will benefit you to learn to live with them. **One method to embrace this type of person involves learning to change your reaction.**
   - You may be used to reacting to this person with anger or frustration. However, if you reacted with calmness and understanding instead, **not only will it put you in control of the interaction, but you might also discover a whole new facet of their personality.**

It is important to keep in mind that even difficult people have feelings and can get hurt. **They need love and understanding just as much or more than anyone else.** Change your reaction to them and you might even gain a new supporter.

COFFEE CHAT WITH HAROUN

The Power of Partnership

HAROUN I've worked for a lot of Non-Governmental Organizations ("NGOs") in many African countries. Having a family from Africa, I've always felt the need to give back to Africa, and contribute to Africa's development. This desire really pushed me into global health because, at first, my undergraduate focus was on healthcare administration in the U.S. healthcare system.

Back in 2013, I was doing program management for the U.S. Centers for Disease Control and Prevention (CDC). The U.S. government helps fund NGOs working to combat HIV and Aids in Zambia, and other low-income countries around the world.

A lot of the program management work I was involved in was making sure that the implementing partners, i.e., NGOs, adhered to the stipulations of the contract or cooperative agreement that they had with the CDC.

Question: How did you share your knowledge in Zambia?

HAROUN I had to make sure that the implementing partners, many of which were local Zambian NGOs, financial books were accurate and managed properly. Once we provided them with a budget ceiling amount, they were to turn in their budget requests, and I had to make sure all their financial records made sense. So, we audited them to make sure everything was in order.

If they requested more funding, or they needed funds for their HIV/AIDS prevention, treatment, and care programming, it would go through me.

Also, the communications person at the time went on maternity leave. My supervisor said, "Oh! We heard you're a good writer ... so we're going to make you the communications person."

So, on top of what I was doing on the program management side, I did the communication stuff. That included writing speeches for the U.S. Ambassador to Zambia.

I also organized events for the CDC. We had an inauguration of our new offices, which I organized and interacted with the media, including contacting the Zambian newspapers, and so forth.

One of the biggest things that I'm proud of is we had a public-private partnership with the Georgian Foundation, which is based in California, four ministries of Zambian government, and Sorenson Forensics. The goal was to reduce the incidence of child sexual abuse through the establishment of an accredited forensic DNA laboratory in the Republic of Zambia.

COLLABORATION

I was tasked to help establish the partnership through facilitating the process of having all partners agree to, and sign, the memorandum of understanding, and also coordinate the culminating event to establish the new lab amongst other partner relationship building duties. In doing this, I had to use my communication, team goal setting, and collaboration skills quite a bit to effectively make sure all the partners knew their roles, and understood how they all contributed to the common goal we were trying to achieve.

I feel that I accomplished a lot in Zambia in my one year there. I could have stayed longer but I wanted some other country experience, so I moved on to Cape Town, South Africa after that.

Question: **Who impacted you in Zambia?**

I was glad to work with the director of CDC-Zambia, and speak more with the Ambassador. However, the person who impacted me the most was the deputy director. He was a Peace Corps volunteer in the beginning of his career, and is a Country Director with the Peace Corps now.

He is an amazing guy, whom I looked up to because he was very knowledgeable, outgoing, highly competent, and a good people-person.

Also, as an African- American male in the global health field, I hadn't seen many African-American males in such a high-level leadership position before, which gave me something to aspire to as well.

I learned a lot from him, like how to run a U.S. mission office, operations, team management, and leadership skills in general. You know, it was good to see another African-American guy in that kind of leadership role. So, I know one day I can get there too.

> **CHALLENGE:**
>
> *Start or join an initiative at school, or, work for a cause that involves team collaboration. Use the career goal chart, record outcomes in the Résumé Builder and use the 3 C's model to navigate team dynamics.*

CHARACTER

It is important to note that character is refined and developed through interaction with other people. Character matures in community. Character stagnates when we isolate ourselves for long periods of time.

Let us talk about the value of service and how serving someone develops our character. We will take a look at a student's fundraising story to see how this works out. I want to encourage you to develop your character because it will sustain your hard work, so you will grow in your career and fulfill your calling in life.

It is a choice.

It is a choice to push past our limitations, to overcome difficult situations, to grace people every single day and not take things personally. It is so easy to get offended. It is so easy to feed our ego and choose selfishness in our choices. However, total disregard for others will always produce a deficit outcome long term.

Bronnie Ware, a nurse and author of *The Top 5 Regrets of the Dying*, recorded the responses of patients in palliative care who were in their last few weeks of life. They never

Character is refined and developed through interaction with other people. Character matures through community.

CHARACTER

mentioned wanting to spend more time in the office, or make a million dollars.

I want you to read the top 5 epiphanies below from her book. These were common themes that surfaced over and over again. Think about their answers and how it pertains to your life currently.

> 1. *I wish I'd had the courage to live a life true to myself, not the life others expected of me.*
> 2. *I wish I hadn't worked so hard.*
> 3. *I wish I'd had the courage to express my feelings.*
> 4. *I wish I had stayed in touch with my friends.*
> 5. *I wish that I had let myself be happier.*

Process your thoughts:

_____

_____

_____

_____

_____

_____

> *Is there is a feeling that you get when you overcome your fear and you take that next step? Please describe it.*
>
> **MICHAEL** *Euphoria. It's joy and happiness and you know, just pleasure that you were able to do something that you previously couldn't or wouldn't. It's really something special and you'll be able to tell all of your friends and family about it at some point.*

COFFEE CHAT WITH MICHAEL TYLER
On Relationships And Fundraising

Question: Can you share about your educational background and your career interest?

MICHAEL Definitely. I'm a student at the University of Richmond where I study Politics and Leadership. I'm in my senior year now, and really like to go into politics or government in order to help people. I really think that's my drive, my passion to help people in the best way that I can. I'm really interested in the way that people live in the cities, the metropolitan areas. I'm interested in housing and education and transportation; those are the things I really care about, and healthcare.

Question: So, how did this opportunity come for you to study abroad?

MICHAEL In the Leadership School, the Jefferson School of Leadership Studies at the University of Richmond, they have partnered with the Richmond School of Law to do a program called Jepson at Cambridge where they send law students, and undergraduates that are in the leadership school, on a five-week study at Emmanuel College, Cambridge University, in the UK.

Question: Why did you choose this program? What was the motivation, the driving force?

MICHAEL I am involved in a lot of organizations on campus, mostly student government. Student government requires that you're on campus in order to be a part of it, and I've become so immersed in committees with members of the administration and committees with other students. These are things I am very passionate about. You're going abroad during the summer to a place like the UK to study something about Law, which is what I'm interested in. Well, it's part of what I'm interested in, so it seemed like a natural fit.

I was able to get the government scholarship called the Gilman International Scholarship, which covered about half of my expenses to go abroad. The government program pays for students who lack funds, but are eligible to go

CHARACTER

abroad, which is incredible. I'm really happy that they were able to support me as well.

Question: **How did you raise the funds to go abroad. What was your fundraising model?**

MICHAEL In the fall, I knew that I was thinking about going abroad the next summer, so the first thing I did was go to the Office of Scholars and Fellowships at my university, and they introduced me to the government scholarship program. They have people that coach you through every step of the process and let you know when the deadlines are.

I submitted my application by the early deadline, which is in November, and I was admitted by February. That was about $4,500 dollars and I knew that the program was about $7,000, excluding the airfare, food, and any kind of money while I'm there. I had to ask family and friends.

I've just been so blessed and fortunate and grateful for all of the support that I received from my family and friends.

Question: **So, what platforms did you use to fundraise?**

MICHAEL One of my friends has been successful with GoFundMe. I've seen that, but mostly, most of my friends I know that were able to get a significant amount of money did so by saving, like from their work, over a period of time.

Most of my money did actually come from relatives; people in the family who were able to support me ... for which reason again, I feel very blessed. But my friend used GoFundMe.

Question: **How important do you think relationships are in helping to raise funds for a goal that you may have? Can you talk about how you built relationships with people over time?**

MICHAEL You'd hope that the people in your family are the ones that want to see you succeed the most, and they do. I've seen that in my personal life – my great aunt, my great uncle, you and your husband, my mom, my God-mom as well.

My grandmother really invested in me going abroad and having this experience, especially, since most of my family has never really studied abroad before in college, and they saw value in me having that experience as part of building a legacy.

So, yes, those relationships with your relatives are very important.

CHARACTER

Question: **But what if you don't necessarily have close family members and supportive relatives? Do you have any advice on building relationships with your peers, mentors, and community?**

MICHAEL A lot of organizations you can join will help you and support you.

Churches will support you a lot of the time, I've seen that with my friends. A lot of organizations that are designed for people from low-income backgrounds or from a variety of backgrounds will also support.

Question: **Did you also write a fundraising letter?**

MICHAEL Yes, and you send letters to your close family and friends. You can also call, but I would advise to try to talk to people in person as much as possible.

> **CHALLENGE:**
>
> *Create a fundraising campaign for a cause, GradPrep's Global Immersion Module, and/or an entrepreneurial endeavor. Design a strategy that will bring in multiple streams of funds from a variety of sources.*

APPENDIX

APPLICATION GUIDE

PERSONAL STATEMENT

1. Be genuine
2. Explain your academic and career goals
3. Tie in why you are a fit within their academic community
4. Explain how you will grow in knowledge and experience, and also how you can contribute to school culture

Assignment

Write your personal statement for one of your school applications.[6]

___

[6] For further resources, visit https://www.usatoday.com/story/college/2012/10/12/10-tips-for-writing-a-grad-school-personal-statement/37398231/

RÉSUMÉ BUILDER

1. Name
2. Address
3. Objective
4. Skills
5. Outcomes (Qualitative and Quantitative)
6. Employer and dates of employment
7. Get four (4) recommenders now (two (2) Academic, two (2) Work Experience)

Tips: Research employer job postings and tailor your objective, cover letter and résumé to highlight the skills they are looking for. Reach out and request an informational interview by phone, or in person. Follow up with a thank you card.

Why this works:

Taking the time to tailor your submission to what they are seeking will set you apart. Additionally, requesting an informational interview beforehand will build a relationship and determine fit. It will show your sincere interest and improve your interviewing skills in the long run.

Assignment:
1. Fill in the Résumé Builder Milestones
2. Design your own Résumé[7]

---

[7] For further resources, visit https://www.uwsuper.edu/career/students/upload/GradRes-Info.pdf

Résumé Builder Milestones

Job / Volunteer / Internship / Fellowship / Work-study

1. Company _____

   Location _____

   Dates Of Employment _____

   Position _____

Skills _____

_____

Qualitative
Outcomes _____

_____

_____

_____

Quantitative
Outcomes _____

_____

_____

_____

| Recommenders |

1. Name _____   2. Name _____

   Phone _____   Phone _____

   Email address _____   Email address _____

Résumé Builder Milestones

Job / Volunteer / Internship / Fellowship / Work-study

1. Company _____

   Location _____

   Dates Of Employment _____

   Position _____

Skills _____
_____

Qualitative
Outcomes _____
_____
_____
_____

Quantitative
Outcomes _____
_____
_____
_____

| Recommenders |

1. Name _____   2. Name _____

   Phone _____   Phone _____

   Email address _____   Email address _____

Résumé Builder Milestones

Job / Volunteer / Internship / Fellowship / Work-study

1. Company _____

   Location _____

   Dates Of Employment _____

   Position _____

Skills _____

_____

Qualitative
Outcomes _____

_____

_____

_____

Quantitative
Outcomes _____

_____

_____

_____

| Recommenders |

1. Name _____   2. Name _____

   Phone _____   Phone _____

   Email address _____   Email address _____

Résumé Builder Milestones

Job / Volunteer / Internship / Fellowship / Work-study

1. Company _____

   Location _____

   Dates Of Employment _____

   Position _____

Skills _____

_____

Qualitative
Outcomes _____

_____

_____

_____

Quantitative
Outcomes _____

_____

_____

_____

Recommenders

1. Name _____   2. Name _____

   Phone _____   Phone _____

   Email address _____   Email address _____

Résumé Builder Milestones

Job / Volunteer / Internship / Fellowship / Work-study

1. Company _____

    Location _____

    Dates Of Employment _____

    Position _____

Skills _____

_____

Qualitative
Outcomes _____

_____

_____

_____

Quantitative
Outcomes _____

_____

_____

_____

_____

| Recommenders |

1. Name _____   2. Name _____

    Phone _____   Phone _____

    Email address _____   Email address _____

Résumé Builder Milestones

Job / Volunteer / Internship / Fellowship / Work-study

1. Company _____

    Location _____

    Dates Of Employment _____

    Position _____

Skills _____

_____

Qualitative
Outcomes _____

_____

_____

_____

Quantitative
Outcomes _____

_____

_____

_____

| Recommenders |

1. Name _____   2. Name _____

    Phone _____   Phone _____

    Email address _____   Email address _____

RECOMMENDER PACKAGE

1. Start six (6) to twelve (12) months building relationships with supervisors, teachers, managers, and peers that can account for your skills and character.
2. Ask two months in advance if they would like to be a recommender for school and/or employment.
3. Send them the recommendation package one (1) month before application deadline.
4. Remind them two (2) weeks beforehand of the deadline.
5. Send them a thank-you gift card afterwards, and/or take them out to lunch.

Recommendation Package Tips:
* Apprise your recommender of what the school/employer is looking for.
* Include your skills and outcomes as it pertains to what the school/employer is looking for.
* In their letter, give two (2) to three (3) examples for each skill your recommender can attest to.

Assignment:
1. Review the recommendation package example.
2. Build your own recommendation package for one of the schools on your list.

CANDIDATE PROFILE PACKET FOR RECOMMENDER

Candidate Name: _____

Graduate Schools I Am Applying To:

1. _____ - emphasis on _____

2. _____ - emphasis on _____

Recommendation Submission Deadline:

1. _____

2. _____

Table Of Contents

1. Example on the structure of a recommendation letter _____

2. Factors that would be helpful to highlight in my recommendation _____

3. Highlights of my work _____

EXAMPLE ON THE STRUCTURE OF A RECOMMENDATION LETTER

Intro Paragraph

Paragraph 1: *Introduce Yourself*
The first paragraph is where you describe yourself, including your title and company. Next, share how long you have known the applicant, and in what capacity. Also, describe the frequency and context of the interaction.

Paragraph 2: *Highlight your overall assessment of the applicant.*
Touch on **three** of the following attributes: leadership, self-confidence, maturity, creativity, motivation, intellect, analytical ability, integrity, quantitative ability, organizational skills, teamwork skills, global perspective, and/or verbal communication skills.

Body of the Letter

Paragraph 3: *Applicant's First Strong Quality*
Describe the applicant's most impactful quality, and support your assessment with a specific anecdote.

    For example, you might say that Kevin always takes initiative. Support your claim with an incident where he formed a liaison team for two divisions within a company. The objective of the team was to streamline past redundant efforts resulting from lack of communication and disconnects between the two departments. (This is a good example, because it also indirectly highlights that he is a team player.)

Paragraph 4-5: *Applicant's Other Strong Qualities*
Again, state your views with specific examples and anecdotes.

Paragraph 6: *Applicant's Weaknesses Or Developmental Needs*
Be sure to show how graduate school will help strengthen their weaknesses. Also, highlight the current efforts the applicant is taking to overcome a weakness, if applicable.

Paragraph 7-8: *Position the applicant for each school*
Describe how you think they will contribute their post-graduate plans, and how the school's curriculum supports their goal.

Conclusion

Last Paragraph: *Strongly relay your support and confidence in the applicant's abilities*

Your closing sentence should state that the Admissions Committee should feel free to contact you for more information. Include your contact information beneath your signature and name.

1. **Factors that would be helpful to highlight in my recommendation**
   Addressing the three (3) qualities below will be helpful when writing the letter of recommendation:

   a) _____

   _____

   b) _____

   _____

   c) _____

   _____

2. Below are highlights of some of my work at _____.
   (If possible, use some of the answers in your Résumé Builder Milestones sheet for this section)

   _____

   _____

   _____

   _____

ESSAYS

1. **Three Themes:** Your application package is your brand. Leave the committee with three (3) themes that they value in their academic culture. Your essays are an opportunity to reinforce why you are a fit.
2. **Proofreader:** Have someone proofread your essays and provide feedback. See if they can identify the three (3) themes in your essays.
3. **Honor Word Count.** Stick to the word count requested, however, there is grace for under 10% of the maximum word count.

Assignment:
Write the essays for one of your school applications.[8]

_____

_____

_____

_____

_____

_____

_____

_____

---

[8] For further resources, visit https://cdn1.sph.harvard.edu/wp-content/uploads/sites/36/2016/06/Writing-a-Graduate-School-Application-Essay-Guide_Nov-20151.pdf

About the Author

Keisha Dawn Sowers, M.P.A., is the founder of GradPrep.

The 501 (c)(3) organization began in 2003 as a support system for business school students, and later evolved to coach all students through life and career moves. Keisha is passionate about connecting with students in an authentic way. She loves to see peoples' eyes light up when they have that "Aha!" moment, while identifying their various callings in life.

Keisha enjoys cooking, writing books, and meeting new people while traveling with her husband, Tim.

About GradPrep

GradPrep is a student incubator for thought, vision, and experience.

Through Global Immersion Modules and Entrepreneur Bootcamps, the program exists, not only to create a safe space for students through the school application process, but also through life's challenging twists and turns. If you enjoyed the challenges in this workbook, and you feel you are a good fit, go to GradPrep.org to apply for our latest adventure.

The national prep program for graduate study

www.ingramcontent.com/pod-product-compliance
Lightning Source LLC
Chambersburg PA
CBHW060327240426
43665CB00047B/2810